A

TURKISH

DICTIONARY

1913 Press
www.1913press.org
1913press@gmail.com

A Turkish Dictionary, by Andrew Wessels ©2017

1913 is a not-for-profit collective. Contributions to 1913 Press
may be tax-deductible.

Manufactured in the oldest country in the world, The United
States of America.

Many thanks to all the artists, from this century and the last, who
made this project possible.

Founder & Editrice: Sandra Doller
Vice-Editor: Ben Doller
Managing Editrix: Adam Bishop
Text and cover design: This Common Place

ISBN: 978-0-9906332-8-0

A

TURKISH

DICTIONARY

FIRST EDITION

ANDREW WESSELS

1913 PRESS

CONTENTS

A
TURKISH
DICTIONARY

From A
To Z

But to COLLECT the WORDS of our language was a task of greater difficulty: the deficiency of dictionaries was immediately apparent; and when they were exhausted, what was yet wanting must be sought by fortuitous and unguided excursions into books, and gleaned as industry should find, or chance should offer it, in the boundless chaos of a living speech.

Samuel Johnson
from *Preface to a Dictionary of the English Language*

Arabesque

to trace the zero
to trace from the cusp of the zero
a glass of rakı — ice — a black cat blind
mother's simple words blind
in the space of the walk
laces interwoven through the cloth
a song
notes of a hat in the street
rain on the hat in the street
a long line of hats
you if you were not asleep

I. &language

the words mote be cosin to the deede
-Geoffrey Chaucer

I'm not sure when or how I awoke, the sounds of a song lingering in the memory of my ears. In the window of my hotel room, I expect to see my face. And the image looking back

                              a mosaic rose set into the exterior wall of the next building.

On the other side of the wall, rooms, and further, far down the hill, the city flows around the Bosporus, the Golden Horn, and sky.

To go to see the water, I count my way down the stairs to the number zero.

I begin with what I see to come
to what I know.

Say Istanbul and a seagull comes to mind...
(Bedri Rahmi Eyuboğlu)

The sky is different here.

To begin.

The Turkish Republic began with a speech.

In 1927, Atatürk addressed the new parliament. To say for the first time *Türkiye*. To say for the first time *İstanbullu*. To say for the first time *a seagull comes to mind.*

In 1932 the Türk Dil Kurumu (Turkish Language Institution) is founded to cleanse the Ottoman language, to create an official Turkish language purged of borrowed words, of grammar, of Arabic script, of Ottoman heritage.

Hundreds of words become alien, then cease.

AİLE :: FAMILY

a table set many ways   my fork
a slower fern grows

latitudes & brief respites deep
breaths for the sake of accumulation

fallen on the crafted stair
falling amid the light of oncoming

stares a visible lineage if you listen
to foucault scallywag & sinner

a table set many ways   my fork
& spoon the wrong side

Today, Atatürk's first speech to parliament has become impenetrable to contemporary Turks, who rely on a series of translations (1964, 1986, 1995) to modernize its language, return it to understandability.

And how did things change?

> iktibas: become: alıntı
> tecessüm: become: görünme
> müellif: become: yazar

Even a month changed: teşrinievvel: become: ekim

                                    but that one makes sense

to purge the language of

To begin to change, first turn the alphabet from Arabic script to Latin letters: left to right, not right to left

                        letters aren't as pretty as

Oh Atatürk, where did you put all those words?

Say Istanbul and a seagull comes to mind
Half-silver and half-foam, half-fish and half-bird.
Say Istanbul and a fable comes to mind,
The old wives' tale that we have all heard.
                                    (Bedri Rahmi Eyuboğlu)

I'm in arms here this wind and

*Say **Istanbul** and a **seagull** comes to mind*
Half-silver and half-foam, half-fish and half-bird.
*Say **Istanbul** and a **fable** comes to mind,*
*The old wives' **tale** that we have all **heard**.*

Istanbul   seagull/Istanbul   fable
          tale   heard

Oh, so many words. Where did they go, Atatürk?

Arkadaş :: Friend

*

tiles laid over the light

*

i refused to believe until i saw

*

seen and now

*

the narrow back street

*

first turn   within the pattern

*

raveling from that

*

look out over the city

*

waters you grew up

*

The bookseller outside the Grand Bazaar brought five versions of Atatürk's speech, *Nutuk*, each edition larger and longer than the last, the last a four-volume set filled with translations and translations of translations

marginalia

etymology

annotations

each more different than
the last. Version piled upon version in which somewhere was an original word.

The first two versions diverged before the fifth word uttered. I asked the bookseller where the original document was held. One must know the name of what one seeks.

Oh, Atatürk, where did they put your words?

BURASI :: THIS PLACE

this apple rolls upon the lawn
excluded middle spun internal these
exclusionary tactics budded leaves far
cry a missed bird silent now miss
the words to say i say apple and
chairs chess-set and nothing
strings out of it simple as two
leaves either side perfect
crisp strip them the vein a single line
intertwined between raindrop and puddle it
rains during the spring even the apple
spun in ground a valley or a peak let me
peek over it see clay mountains deep
lakes photographs in the lobby
stop for a moment look
a dream turns a puff of apple
flavored smoke the crest a wave bit

Nutuk begins:

1335 senesi Mayısının 19 uncu günü Samsuna çıktım. Vaziyet ve manzarai umumiye:

Osmanlı Devletinin dahil bulunduğu grup, Harbi Umumîde mağlûp olmuş, Osmanlı ordusu her tarafta zedelenmiş, şeraiti ağır, bir mütarekename imzalanmış. Büyük Harbin uzun seneleri zarfında, millet yorgun ve fakir bir halde. Millet ve memleketi Harbi Umumîye sevkedenler, kendi hayatları endişesine düşerek, memleketten firar etmişler. Saltanat ve hilâfet mevkiini işgal eden Vahdettin, mütereddi, şahsını ve yalnız tahtını temin edebileceğini tahayyül ettiği denî tedbirler araştırmakta. Damat Ferit Paşanın riyasetindeki kabine; âciz, haysiyetsiz, cebîn, yalnız padişahın iradesine tâbi ve onunla beraber şahıslarını vikaye edebilecek herhangi bir vaziyeti razı.

Ordunun elinden esliha ve cephanesi alınmış ve alınmakta...

İtilâf Devletleri, mütareke ahkâmına riayete lüzum görmüyorlar. Birer vesile ile, İtilâf donanmaları ve askerleri İstanbulda. Adana vilâyeti, Fransızlar; Urfa, Maraş, Ayıntap, İngilizler tarafından işgal edilmiş. Antalya ve Konyada, İtalyan kıtaatı askeriyesi; Merzifon ve Samsunda İngiliz askerleri bulunuyor. Her tarafta, ecnebî zabit ve memurları ve hususî adamları faaliyette. Nihayet, mebdei kelâm kabul ettiğimiz tarihten dört gün evvel, 15 Mayıs 1335 de İtilâf Devletlerinin muvafakatile Yunan ordusu İzmire ihraç ediliyor...

Within five years, *Nutuk* becomes:

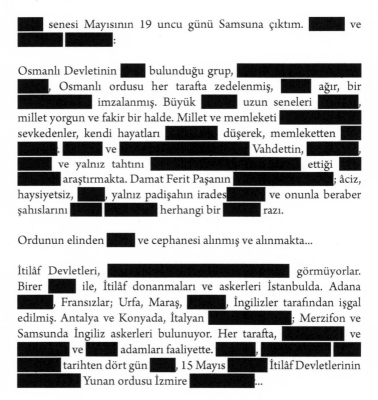

███ senesi Mayısının 19 uncu günü Samsuna çıktım. ██████ ve
███████ ████████:

Osmanlı Devletinin ███ bulunduğu grup, ██████████████████
███████, Osmanlı ordusu her tarafta zedelenmiş, ████ ağır, bir
████████████ imzalanmış. Büyük ████ uzun seneleri ██████,
millet yorgun ve fakir bir halde. Millet ve memleketi ███████
sevkedenler, kendi hayatları █████████ düşerek, memleketten ███
███████. ████ ve ████████████████ Vahdettin, ██████████,
██████ ve yalnız tahtını ██████████████████ ettiği ████
██████ araştırmakta. Damat Ferit Paşanın ████████████; âciz,
haysiyetsiz, ████, yalnız padişahın irades████ ve onunla beraber
şahıslarını ████ ███████ herhangi bir ████ razı.

Ordunun elinden ████ ve cephanesi alınmış ve alınmakta...

İtilâf Devletleri, ███████████████████████████ görmüyorlar.
Birer ████ ile, İtilâf donanmaları ve askerleri İstanbulda. Adana
███████, Fransızlar; Urfa, Maraş, ███████, İngilizler tarafından işgal
edilmiş. Antalya ve Konyada, İtalyan ████████████; Merzifon ve
Samsunda İngiliz askerleri bulunuyor. Her tarafta, ██████████ ve
███████████ ve ████ adamları faaliyette. ██████, ██████████
████████ tarihten dört gün ███, 15 Mayıs ████ İtilâf Devletlerinin
██████████ Yunan ordusu İzmire ████████...

yaptırtılamayabilir can be translated as 'it may not possibly be made to be done'

how much can we store in a single word?

how much can we store in a single word?

ÇEŞME   ::   FOUNTAIN, WELL

*

dangled legs close

*

new day turns red in this wind

*

keep that window open longer

*

streams haphazard stones

*

the prayer itself a call to prayer

*

this long broadway this wind this salt a sun

*

i am   hear further now

*

Born one year before the founding of the Turkish Language Institution, the Turkish poet Ece Ayhan became the streets of Istanbul just like Rimbaud in Paris. *Flâneur* become *avare*.

In the re-printing of the English translation of his two books *Bakışsız Bir Kedi Kara* and *Ortodoksluklar* as the single volume *A Blind Cat Black and Orthodoxies*, "Ece Ayhan takes the reader through the dark streets of the Galata district of Istanbul in these gay-inspired poems. Like a modern-day Rimbaud, Ayhan explores linguistically and thematically what Turkish culture and authorities have forbidden."

And a description of Ayhan as author: "A gay author, Ece Ayhan was one of Turkey's most noted poets, living in the red-light district of Istanbul."

To walk these streets and see.

One of Ayhan's poems looks like this:

"Sentez"   "Synthesis"

Şu taşbasması   This lithograph
İşkence Usülleri kitabı   –the book of the codes of torture–
Nerede basma iş   Where the impression is work
Babil'de   At Babel
Babil'de bir çocuk demek At Babel a child says
Bizi kullanıp kullanıp duruyormuş It stops us again and again
Ama biz bu değiliz ki   But we are not this which
Daha ilk sayfalarda   Until now on these first pages
Karşımıza çıkıveriyor   Emerging from our opposite
Başkasının gözleri   Your other eyes
Başkasının ağızları dudakları Your other mouths, lips
Babil'de basılmış   At Babel are printed
Birer birer açılan   Opening one by one
Hayatımıza.   Our life.

Now walk into this city, see, hear, and speak. Begin.

I begin.

Bird.

Only, bird.

Only:

Bird(s).

A bird. Some birds.

DOĞRU :: CORRECT, TRUE, FAITHFUL

*

every thing back to the surface

*

this carapace better than before

*

soon i will wake and again be with you

*

than the tendril a bifurcation   rain   contact

*

light played in a thousand drops

*

Yes, now. Now, a bird. Now I think, a little bit, of a bird. But what of what bird?

A bird flies.

And I begin again.

> A bird flies
> and dives, probably after
> an insect that can't be seen—too
> small you know—nearly skims
> the cement walkway bordered by grass
> on one side desert on the other
> pulls up and alights
> (is it light out?)
> on the branch of some tree.

Yes, now I see.

Now a bird that flies, that dives, that pulls up, that alights (if it is light out?).

Ev :: House

*

who breaks sunlight into

*

seen above and now

*

blue   curls ceiling to floor

*

how high go bird nests

*

the current   wind come still on their backs

*

A bird flies
and dives, probably after
an insect that can't be seen—too
small you know—nearly skims
the cement walkway bordered by grass
on one side desert on the other
pulls up and alights
(is it light out?)
on the branch of some tree.

What part is necessary?

A **bird** flies
and dives, probably **after**
an **insect** that can't be seen—too
small you know—nearly **skims**
the **cement** walkway bordered by **grass**
on one side **desert** on the other
pulls up and alights
(is it light out?)
on the **branch** of some tree.

Gökyüzü   ::   Sky, Sphere, The Heavens

*

used piece of equipment

*

open space itself edge the city further

*

blue and white on blue edges

*

closer expanse   conspiracy   space

*

warmth turn and run light on light

*

the center   puddles

*

bird   after insect
seen skims
cement   grass/desert   other
branch

İLKBAHAR   ::   FIRST SPRING

The cloud of word is cloud.
The color of word is white
clean pure ominous. The wind
so away—

Pigeon feathers in the parking lot.
Blue varieties.
A new civilization. A blue
seagull across the window.

The statue bronze and greening, the hand
stretches up at the ceiling, the world
moss metal inside.

The waters flow past the prophet's footprint.
The view tonight is so rare.

to begin:

> i knew they were birds
> every way the rock here
> red from the street and red
> from up close a suggestion

to become:

> i know
> birds
> rock
> farther
> from
> away
> farther
> still

II. & history

The past is always present: one need only make up one's mind to go there.
-Nicolas Bourriaud

Burada   Orada

Here   &   There

        these men stand here on the edge of the bridge for
                stood here for

            these men sit here on the edge of the bridge for
                      sat here for

twenty tiny fish pulled up equals a meal

        for what is stood for

KALABALIK :: CROWDED

i moved::the road is dry and crusty the rains come in the spring and the birds the leaves let go this hand the burning::a seat five feet from your right next to each other this leaf falls for hours the sound of a cricket once::tall grasses brushed::let go this hand the burning::the funny thing is::a daisy is your favorite they grow here::and let go this hand the burning::the words are ferry water shore button cow and sun::an olive covered with white wine::the space between beef and cow a matter of taste and cigarettes::let go this hand the burning::face the crowd straight a show of grace::in this city there is in this city there is in this city there is::rain on these stones::little red thing when humor collides::an open door

I crossed the Galata Bridge linking the new city to the old city and listened to
the sounds of ferries
>   water against boat
>   people
>   redirected wind
>   chains
>   horns
>   the chiming of numerous small bells
>   that sailed by on both
sides, carrying people across the Golden Horn and up the throat of the
Bosporus to branch out into the city's sprawl.

Near the top of a steep but walkable hill rests the Istanbul that was fought over. Sitting in what is now a developed square next to a park centered by a fountain between the Hagia Sophia and Blue Mosque, I seek the city that was. I watch as the Blue Mosque, which had not yet arrived, disappears and the Hippodrome, marked now by three lone pillars crawling up through the square around me, rises. The endless rows of restaurants, tourist depots, and *lokum* shops released from their buildings, reclaimed by time.

This is the city that was killed over, the Hagia Sophia rising up to look out over Horn and Throat. The museum returns to mosque then cathedral then large red building against the blue sky.[*]

---

[*] On January 12, 2016, approximately five and a half years after considering these thoughts, a suicide bomber detonated himself next to the Obelisk of Theodosius a few yards from the bench where I sat in the Hippodrome's former center. Fourteen people, including the bomber, died. When I sit on this bench again today, other than a small, makeshift flowerpot memorial that is filled primarily with rainwater, there is no trace of the blast on the stones set in the ground or the obelisk itself, which stands as if untouched.

As I later discovered in *The Patria*—a history of Constantinople compiled in the tenth century by an unknown author threading together myths, legends, and the accounts of various and contradictory preceding texts—the Hagia Sophia was founded for the following reason:

> *In the fifth year of the reign of Justinian the Great, after the massacre had happened in the Hippodrome—thirty-five thousand were killed there, because the two circus factions had proclaimed as emperor Hypatios, the patrician and faction leader of the Blues —so in the fifth year of his reign God inspired him to build a church such as had never been built since Adam's time.*

KİTAP :: BOOK

At my desk,
in my tradition. There's a lamp
beside me and light
comes in from the kitchen. It rained
and now, dry, neighbors
check their mail. The purpose
of this book is to explain
the vagaries of a poet. The prose
a vagary itself, though I try
to make sense. I wanted things
to be better, and for a time
the sun will continue to shine. From
England to China there is so much
room for a word to break. It rained
and now, dry, head off.

When restoring the badly degraded structure in the 19th Century, the Fossati brothers recorded inscriptions etched onto the walls of the Hagia Sophia after the earthquake of 869.

Lining the northern dome it was written:

Time has threatened to destroy this inimitable work;
it has been hindered by our solicitude.
Do Thou open unto me Thy house,
O Most High Lord, which time toucheth not.

Centuries before the fall (taking) of Constantinople, fellow Christians destroyed the original mosaics decorating the Hagia Sophia walls. Iconoclasts seeking walls stripped to bareness.

After Istanbul became, Ottoman guidelines ensured the preservation of the replaced mosaic walls under a film of plaster, never meant to be seen again but still existing. Where they are now slowly uncovering:

LEKE :: STAIN, SPOT

halfway down
the broken
staircase wandered
through

brightness of flame
lasting
how fruit
hung aloft by chains

leaves
radiant heavens
in the great
apparition

until he
acts as scaffolding
truth
rests

on immeasurable air
great helmet
why floods
grope

among dry bones
washed across
my toenails
under this

journey through
them
its better
in the park

Today, visitors are politely asked to refrain from using flash photography. The Virgin Mary and Christ Child shout at them from the apse:

> *The images which the impostors*
> *had formerly cast down*
> *here pious emperors have again set up.*

To find what I seek I must accept what is available. I must accept the rate at which information degrades as time carries it forward, away from its source.

According to the list of "Epoch-Making Events" in the *Nuttall Encyclopedia: Being a Concise and Comprehensive Dictionary of Knowledge*, the fall (taking) of Constantinople by Mehmed II/Mahomet II/el-Fatih/the Conqueror in 1453 occurred just before Columbus' discovery of America and just following the invention of the printing press, here dated 1436 though elsewhere one finds other dates.

ÖTESİ :: WHAT FOLLOWS, BEYOND

one day was the first day
                    cool and a question of
          perspiration on the tabletop
                    the new building set stone over stone
          among tall weeds next to the river
                    on the ground lost with the bugs
               a daydream of spiders in the snow

one day was the second day
                    dim and windy
          blocked by the last rays of sun
                         a mutual tower
crisp mint and fantastic women

                    i've been having this trouble
                         your hat
          upside down and perched over
the staircase
                    the unique marks
          of teeth on my skin
our names graffitied
                    onto matchbooks
lean me westward
                         a stalk of tall grass
          around my index finger
the purpling of the tip

                    this trouble with
                         a white stone
          chalky in my hand
                    when i draw a flower or a bird

According to the entry on "Printing" from the second volume of *Lexicon Technicum: Or, An Universal English Dictionary of Arts and Sciences: Explaining not only the Terms of Art, but the Arts Themselves*, editor John Harris dates the possible founding of the printing press at 1430, an invention made more efficient by Gutenberg and paper *made of Linnen Rags first made at Basil, by some Greeks, who fled out of their country after Constantinople was sackt, A.D. 1452.*

The same entry includes a story about John Fust, an assistant to the early printer Laurenzi Koster, who stole his master's tools and absconded to Mentz. Fust then headed to Paris loaded down with printed Bibles, selling them as if they were manuscripts, which means really written by hand.

The Bibles' conformity revealed him, each letter too much like every other
letter *throughout the whole, to a Line, a Word, a Letter, nay even to a Point*
mistakes either consistent or nonexistent. Which caused, to no surprise, great
alarm, allegations of magical feats, unnatural creation.

                                          The entry tells us
John Fust became later known as *Faust* or *Faustus*, consort of Helen of Troy
and the devil himself. Became the man creating a mythology from an act of
recreation

                to fill the world with the same thing, the words printed again and
again.

Set into the stone floor on the upper level of the Hagia Sophia rests a single nameplate stamped with a single name:

Born in Venice (1107), died in Constantinople (1205), buried in the Hagia Sophia. Between, became the Doge of Venice and led the Crusade to take Constantinople from the other Christians.

This is his tomb, which lasted the fall (taking) of Constantinople, the birth of Istanbul, the fall of the Ottoman Empire, the creation of the Turkish Republic.

This tomb that contains no bones.

SES :: VOICE

*

spun along the wall a row books eyed perched

*

let me find   your words faint

*

some thing we hear elsewhere now offers

*

last man standing paint blue above cold

*

talk out of arms legs red shirts

*

sound of water   come closer sheer light

*

outside the window activity spun from wires twists of fingers

*

To find what I seek in what cannot be seen.

I traveled to Ankara to see Atatürk's body. The city he created in the center of the country he created.

Seeing Atatürk's tomb asks for faith.

His body is visited by climbing Rasattepe hill to the Anıtkabir monument. From the top of the hill, I find myself in the middle of Ankara watching the entire city grow. For Atatürk to keep watch over his country.

I allow myself to be overwhelmed by the vaulted ceilings in the ceremonial stone mausoleum, Atatürk's place of rest marked by a forty ton sarcophagus.

This sarcophagus that contains no bones.

In a basement seven meters directly below the sarcophagus, deep within the hill, sits an octagonal room. In the center of the room, a long, red marble stone erupts from the floor, surrounded by eighty-one jars filled with dirt collected from eighty-one Turkish cities. Atatürk's body rests underneath this stone. I can see none of these things.

A small television screen blocks the doorway into this tomb. The screen plays a live feed of the interior of the tomb, the camera's lens rotating to show the marble in the floor and the gold mosaic sunburst on the ceiling. I must accept the image on the screen.

The end of the educational documentary *Anıtkabir Belgeseli* purports to show the tomb behind the screen. The immense, ornately carved door begins to swing outward to reveal the interior. The moment before the tomb comes into view, the film cuts to black before reappearing to show a different set of double doors opening inward into the tomb. The original door, screen, and exterior room have vanished. I follow the camera's eye into this new room because I must, or else turn away to something else.

SIR   ::   SECRET, MYSTERY

The strangely dark house prepared
to wait for morning's strike along
its carved siding. The clouds
dried up above and revealed
one bright star in the sky.
Beyond that, the sea and out
further another country, continent
so far away. In this land

the squares rested beneath
the multitudes, the stones shifting
to meet the people succumbing
to the pull of gravity. One year ago
or one year later, when the order
came to march, they left the cities
of their grandfathers' deaths, the lights

at home still on at their backs. That first
evening was altitude, only
thinking of the blood coursing
through the throat, looking out upon
this overbuilt city, the distance
between the sound of the waves.

To become witness to his death, the eye must accept the image on the screen. How we are remembered. How we are saved. How we are differentiated from the earth we return to.

Oh Atatürk, where did they put your bones?

& history & language & let's make this concrete how can I understand?

On October 10, 2009 in Zurich, the foreign ministers from Turkey and
Armenia signed an accord to normalize relations between the two nations.

& Henricus (Enrico) Dandolo spoke Latin & was the Doge from Venice &
in old age led the Fourth Crusade & sacked Constantinople & even to got
to revel (for a short while) in his conquest before he was buried in the Hagia
Sophia built by Emperor Justinian

Shortly after the Zurich meeting, the mayor of Kars, a small city that sits near
the Turkish-Armenian border, commissioned the artist Mehmet Aksoy to
build a 30 meter high statue on a hill just outside the city, a statue to be seen
from Armenia.

ŞİMDİLİK :: FOR THE PRESENT, TEMPORARILY

*

among long grasses

*

it can be fun underneath

*

start again a different order

*

a star   again   finds new order

*

single bed we sleep our clothes on

*

& there's a nameplate claiming Henricus' resting place & it might be real though the nameplate itself probably isn't & it made you think (made me think): in war the mutual appreciation between war & warred / infidel & infidel

In January 2011, as the statue was nearing completion, the Turkish Prime Minister Recep Tayyip Erdoğan visited Kars. During his tour of the city, he headed to the outskirts to view the giant statue being constructed. Upon gazing at the two stone figures depicted thrusting their hands toward each other, hoping to make contact, Erdoğan immediately ordered the removal of İnsanlık Anıtı, the *Statue of Humanity*.

In April 2011 work began to erase the sculpture from the hillside.

Or maybe there just wasn't time to extract his bones just dust anyway

"Mr. Erdoğan insisted that his taste was purely aesthetic ... *Two vast and ugly blocks of stone*"
                    - *The Economist*

SONBAHAR   ::   LAST SPRING, FALL

I go loud into this shouting stone
once for the clock lost in the grass and once
until I return home. These briars in my pocket
keep spring next to my thigh when the clouds break
to the stars all this must go into safekeeping.

Winter leans in the sky that can only be called
that thing above us. Look at how we see it, how we
can't raise ourselves as if we would really want to.
As if there is anything more than ground, more than
the joy of sitting together on the couch. The experiment

went well, counting the odd number of cows we stopped
next to on the highway to take photographs of landscape
and occasion, the way the road reminded us of a movie
or another photograph or conversation or dream
we shared until we recognized it before us. Red rock

shoved up from earth. Last night we made fire
slept in the back of the car. I remember different things
from this time, the texture of the wood or the height
of the ancient walls, what it was like to be, to be in it
on the brink of the world life an exploration.

or, as Barbaro the Venetian surgeon reports:

> *The blood flowed in the city like rainwater in the gutters*
> *after a sudden storm, and the corpses of Turks and Christians*
> *were thrown into the Dardanelles, where they floated out to*
> *sea like melons along a canal.*

III. &faith

Of course, the phenomenology of a rich visual world is undeniable.
-Michael Cohen & Daniel Dennett

I saw the world and yet I was not seen
-Chidiock Tichborne

To intertwine this and this

Blue the name of color

To interlace this and this

Red the throat of color

To interlay this and this

Green the life of color

To interweave this and this

White the cloud of color

From pagan to a different pagan, from a different pagan to Christian, from Christian to a different Christian, from a different Christian to Muslim, from Muslim to Western Secularist.

From a name lost to the past to Byzantium to Constantinople to Istanbul where I sit as the city re-builds itself around me.

I watch the Hippodrome erased back to its current state of ruin. As it falls, the Blue Mosque's six minarets stretch themselves up toward the sky, and the surrounding shops, homes, restaurants, hotels, and people ebb and flow until I find myself again surrounded by what appears here before me.

SORU :: QUESTION

*

prayer sung awake at four

*

take this throat in hand

*

i am found on the backside of this

*

i am found with you in the same city

*

we are to go beyond

*

i am found minarets through your palm

*

the gypsy stole the honeypot the gypsy stole   arrest!

*

i am found coffee grounds spread out against

*

i am found stop i am stop i

*

I walk back, following the winding streets back down the hill back to the water back across the bridge back up to my hotel room where I lay myself down to rest.

In the cool darkness of the room I look at a map of the city to trace my meandering. Though I cannot say for certain which streets I followed, my finger traces one possible route through the city then another then another then faster through the city between the buildings up and down the hills past all the people, places, things. The possible routes infinite within this small square of space. My path one possible arabesque through the city and then another and then.

There's always a mistake.

Even in the most intricately planned and designed mosque or palace, there's always a mistake. A part of the algorithm guiding the designer's hand is ignored momentarily and the mosaic's pattern ceases to be infinite symmetry. One edge of the motif bleeds too far into the next, one color used for another.

The mistakes could be the inevitable typo in the expansive, increasingly complicated mathematical designs stretching from floor to ceiling.

Many believe, though, that the mistakes are purposeful: the designer's acknowledgment that only the one creator above can achieve perfection. That the reality of living in our world is inherent imperfection.

That there is always a mistake here among us.

That we always mistake.

Though I can never be certain why these mistakes exist in general or why a specific mistake appears in a particular design, I can choose to believe that it is only *through the mediation of such drawings that one can begin to penetrate the language of geometric design.*

The language within the geometric design. The language within the failure. The language in the art. The language in the math. The language in the language.

One and one makes.

SURET :: DUPLICATE, REPRESENTATION, FIGURE

*

list along the diagonal

*

in what directions one should

*

to mind simultaneously suggested   given

*

the copyist clear in other

*

the early point   the smaller square

*

stand for one and one in order drawn

*

every detail two distinct

*

these all we   proceed   remain

*

As I trace each potential route through the city, I find myself humming the theme to Steve Reich's "Piano Phase."

In the piece, two pianos play in tandem the same scale over and over and over again: *Duh-duh-duh-DUH-duh-duh Duh-duh-duh-DUH-duh-duh*. At defined intervals, one piano speeds up momentarily to move one note ahead of its partner in the scale, then another, then another, until finally, the phases complete, the two pianos are returned to unified play.

Let me do the same thing this way. And this way. And now this way, too. And this. The same thing, again, anew. Each thing each way until it fills me into the next.

In another of Reich's compositions, "Proverb," five choral singers repeat the same line over and over and over again, a line borrowed from Ludwig Wittgenstein:

How small a thought it takes to fill a whole life!

The song repeats itself I am myself awake listening
                                                        thinking
                                                                        the thought that must

And on the other side of the window, the mosaic rose. I press the map against the window to trace the rose's form, letting its way guide my own way through the city. This is what I did and this is what I will do and this is my life

that my

life, this

In *Tractatus Logico-Philosophicus*, Wittgenstein uses the word "life" ten times:

3.323   In the language of everyday **life** it very often happens
that the same word signifies in two different ways—
and therefore belongs to two different symbols—or
that two words, which signify in different ways, are
apparently applied in the same way in the proposition.

TANIŞMAK :: TO MEET

When I looked up from the arabesque
        to the sun's stream spreading itself
across the carpet where I kneeled surrounding
        me heat grass appropriating my limbs
the face appeared through the room
        steady above me gently approaching
a touch to my side. Bid me exit. Understand
        what is both in and around me, alone
unseen, searching for the mistake that would
        complete the search. I held steady
two inches away, the pattern consuming me
        for two hours tracing the meander
with the tip of my tongue, my finger,
        my eye the precision instrument
guided at last briefly at last hidden
        behind the pillar. The air wavered
into land and water, people building
        lives in the scrub. Sit over the water

5.621   The world and **life** are one.

TANIŞMAK   ::   TO MEET

breathe the world that comes
            together. Wind clears the smoke and men
pull up small fish in loaves of bread.
            How stone is rock and fire
freedom matching the spread of people
            to stars crafting mythos to understand
the simple things: first feet
            used to shift the boat's balance
drifting among the boats. When the words
            to call are few and strict, language
a clock tweaked past spring and two
            birds are one to fill this place
with call and call. *This was the Promised*
            Land and it still is exactly what it was
before. Pillar before me speak.
            The tendril snakes its way through
skin, my throat an open tendril
            turns blue across red, the taste

6.211   In **life** it is never a mathematical proposition which we need, but we use mathematical propositions only in order to infer from propositions which do not belong to mathematics to others which equally do not belong to mathematics.

Tanışmak :: To Meet

of iron set in stone. *So we must*
        from the hawk's far stemming view
sit in the shade and drink tea
        from tulips. This curve sings next
to the metrobus station. That border
        carries the crowd shifting
through traffic's obedient madness
        crossing the gravity that counteracts
the weight of gravity, pulling back
        against the water. Look at the bridge
tell me you can see the same thing
        different as it must be.
Remember the occasion then
        wander off into winding streets
our *ripe fields revolving*
        through their harvests in sweet torment.
So many are something
        else entirely, the amount of blood we lose

6.4311   Death is not an event of **life**. Death is not lived through. If by eternity is understood not endless temporal duration but timelessness, then he lives eternally who lives in the present.

Our **life** is endless in the way that our visual field is without limit.

TANIŞTIRMAK   ::   TO INTRODUCE

in death, how it eventually
          hardens too. My note mimicked Twombly:
Irresponsibility of Gravity. Red
          loops hanging in the wings. Intimate
writings too large or condensed
          or considered, too magnified
or diffuse, too red to mean
          what I viewed. Look through me
dear editor, consider this accompanying
          manuscript entitled "Consciousness
cannot be separated from function."
          To illustrate this point a hypothetical
"perfect experiment" is proposed
          completely isolated from the subject,
the experimenter, and science itself.
          Below are names. Apple. Street. Grass.
Pigeon. Window. Train. Minaret.
          Book. Vine. Whether the apple is red

6.4312   The temporal immortality of the soul of man, that is to say, its eternal survival also after death, is not only in no way guaranteed, but this assumption in the first place will not do for us what we always tried to make it do. Is a riddle solved by the fact that I survive for ever? Is this eternal **life** not as enigmatic as our present one? The solution of the riddle of **life** in space and time lies outside space and time.

(It is not problems of natural science which have to be solved.)

TANIŞTIRMAK :: TO INTRODUCE

is red with you in your palm. Where
            the call to prayer is the paper dove
on the horizon. Where the sky
            can be touched, where it presses down
among us, sliver of ghosts
            piled among ghosts. We are old
meat thrown among purple flowers,
            tomato vines, imprint of feet held up
against the sky. We are an indulgent strip
            of heat across the balcony. This figure I see
closed and infinite in nature is the leftovers
            the revolutions of our eyes
around the pupil, the iris,
            invisible blood vessels. I passed through
the gateway leading out of the mosque's complex.
            The first words called me across the city. What it is
to know these words. Watch it grow the grass
            the world that is full of when clouds break.

6.52 We feel that even if all possible scientific questions be answered, the problems of **life** have still not been touched at all. Of course there is then no question left, and just this is the answer.

VAR :: EXISTENT

Whether I am stone or iron I will be brought
back to life, sailed in on ships from sea, led in
through the gates. To be a tree is to be a tree: green
scissored into leaves turning too slow to catch up.

The first time was better, two bodies orbiting,
depending on the counteracting weight of the other.
Which means love when it's read closely. Love
isn't that at all, what it means to be real. I must
do something wrong, these vibrations in the air

follow the embankment away from water
up to dusk where hands touch the story
starts far away.

6.521   The solution of the problem of **life** is seen in the vanishing of this problem.

(Is not this the reason why men to whom after long doubting the sense of **life** became clear, could not then say wherein this sense consisted?)

YOK   ::   NOT EXISTENT

in the elation

the moon
gibbous is funny

servant perhaps or standard

bearer
burnt rosewood
bored

tree-fin better yet red

slate counter
functional static

the moon stands funny

wind
function
bored in red

bored by burnt counter or

tree-fin yet
better

standard bearer standing

he laughs
gibbous
whistle

unsettled we know it round

mountain gibbous
moonlight peek

what is a tree-fin he asks

wind
born standing
yet

we stood in the elation

under gibbous
laughed at hollow

a better servant perhaps

        others full
        wind
        burning

better yet he laughs

        tree-fin a
        round

the servant has a tell

        red wind
        mountain
        gibbous moon

standing in the elation

        word in sand
        moon through wind

At 3:37 I wake myself to hear the call to prayer.

I think my name lying on the covers of my hotel bed as the prayer arrives, calling me to prepare for my own act of prayer.

My eye and ear, my tongue and finger.

I count my way.

Sources

- Talat S. Halman's *A Brave New Quest: 100 Modern Turkish Poems* (Syracuse University Press)
- Geoffrey L. Lewis's *Turkish Grammar* (Oxford University Press) and *The Turkish Language Reform: A Catastrophic Success* (OUP)
- Aslı Göksel and Celia Kerslake's *Turkish: A Comprehensive Grammar* (Routledge)
- Ece Ayhan's *Bütün Yort Savul'lar!: Toplu Şiirler 1954-1997* (Yapı Kredi Yayınları)
- Natalia Teteriatnikov's "Hagia Sophia, Constantinople: Religious Images and their Functional Context after Iconoclasm" (*Zograf* 2004)
- Albrecht Brechter's translation of *The Patria* (Harvard University Press)
- Ralph Waldo Emerson's "Nature" (1836)
- Procopius of Caesarea's "On the Great Church" and Paul the Silentiary's "The Magnificence of Hagia Sophia" from W.R. Lethaby and Harold Swainson's *The Church of St Sophia Constantinople* (Macmillan & Co)
- *The Nuttall Encyclopædia: Being a Concise and Comprehensive Dictionary of Knowledge* (Frederick Warne & Co Ltd)
- John Harris's *Lexicon Technicum: Or, An Universal English Dictionary of Arts and Sciences: Explaining not only the Terms of Art, but the Arts Themselves*
- Nicolo Barbaro's *Diary of the Siege of Constantinople 1453* translated by J.R. Jones (Exposition Press)
- W.K. Chorbachi's "In the Tower of Babel: Beyond Symmetry in Islamic Design" (*Computers Math. Applic.* 1989)
- Ludwig Wittgenstein's *Tractatus Logico-Philosophicus* translated by C.K. Ogden
- Hart Crane's *The Bridge* (Library of America)
- Michael Cohen and Daniel Dennett's "Consciousness cannot be separated from function" (*Trends in Cognitive Sciences* 2011)

ACKNOWLEDGEMENTS

This book could not have been written without the many who have pushed me and held me up over the years. Thank you to the editors of *580 Split*, *Spiral Orb*, *summer stock*, *VOLT*, and *Witness* for publishing selections from this work. Thank you to my mentors Don Revell, Claudia Keelan, and Molly Bendall. To my UNLV companions, for our community and our nights at the Frog. To my family—Mom, Dad, Grace, Evan—for helping me see how to wander. To the amazing collective at 1913 for believing that this could and should be a book. To Poets & Writers as well as John Cobain and the Black Mountain Institute for the invaluable support that helped me continue my work. To my friends and colleagues in İstanbul, who welcomed me fully. To the many who have shared their thoughts and conversation throughout these years of journeying and writing, including: Kelli Noftle, Steph Wall, Nurduran Duman, Srikanth Reddy, Dan Beachy-Quick, Andy Fitch, Teresa Carmody, James Meetze, Michael Cohen, Tom Raworth, Emily Motzkus, Mark Irwin, Margaret Rhee, Jamie Asaye FitzGerald, Cheryl Klein, Julian Smith-Newman, Diana Arterian, Brett Zehner, Elisabeth Houston, Lezlie Mayers, Whitney Holmes, Nik De Dominic, and Ryan Winet. To Cody Todd: I wouldn't have made it this far without you.

And, most of all, Zeliha: this one is for you, from you, to you, with you.

About the Author

Andrew Wessels currently splits his time between İstanbul and Los Angeles. Previously, he lived in Houston, Cambridge, and Las Vegas. *Semi Circle*, a chapbook of his translations of the Turkish poet Nurduran Duman, was published by Goodmorning Menagerie in 2016. *A Turkish Dictionary* is his first book.

Titles from 1913 Press:

A Turkish Dictionary by Andrew Wessels (Editrixes' Pick, 2017)
More Plays On Please by Chet Weiner (Assless Chaps, 2016)
Gray Market by Krystal Languell (2016)
I, Too, Dislike It by Mia You (2016, Editrice's Pick)
Arcane Rituals from the Future by Leif Haven (2016, selected by Claudia Rankine)
Unlikely Conditions by Cynthia Arrieu-King & Hillary Gravendyk (2016)
Abra by Amaranth Borsuk & Kate Durbin (2016)
Pomme & Granite by Sarah Riggs (2015)
Untimely Death is Driven Out Beyond the Horizon by Brenda Iijima (2015)
Full Moon Hawk Application by CA Conrad (Assless Chaps, 2014)
Big House/Disclosure by Mendi & Keith Obadike (2014)
Four Electric Ghosts by Mendi & Keith Obadike (2014)
O Human Microphone by Scott McFarland (2014, selected by Rae Armantrout)
Kala Pani by Monica Mody (2013)
Bravura Cool by Jane Lewty (2012, selected by Fanny Howe)
The Transfer Tree by Karena Youtz (2012)
Conversities by Dan Beachy-Quick & Srikanth Reddy (2012)
Home/Birth: A Poemic by Arielle Greenberg & Rachel Zucker (2011)
Wonderbender by Diane Wald (2011)
Ozalid by Biswamit Dwibedy (2010)
Sightings by Shin Yu Pai (2007)
Seismosis by John Keene & Christopher Stackhouse (2006)
Read 1-6, an annual anthology of inter-translation, Sarah Riggs & Cole Swensen, eds.
1913 a journal of forms, Issues 1-6, Sandra Doller, ed.

Forthcoming:

x/she: stardraped by Laura Vena (selected by John Keene)
Lucy 72 by Ronaldo V. Wilson
Umbilical Hospital by Vi Khi Nao
Old Cat Lady: A Love Story in Possibilities by Lily Hoang
Conversations Over Stolen Food by Jon Cotner & Andy Fitch
Dreaming of Ramadi in Detroit by Aisha Sloan (selected by Maggie Nelson)
On Some HispanoLuso Miniaturists by Mark Faunlagui (selected by Ruth Ellen Kocher)
Playing Monster :: Seiche by Diana Arterian (Editrixes' Pick)
Strong Suits by Brad Flis
Hg, the liquid by Ward Tietz

1913 titles are distributed by Small Press Distribution: www.spdbooks.org